Creative
Methods for
Adult
Classes

Creative
Methods for
Adult
Classes

by
John McKinley

 The Bethany Press
St Louis, Mo

Contents

Introduction

This book is a valuable contribution to the literature of adult education and deserves a wide use by workers in this field. It should prove especially helpful in the educational work of the churches.

Until recently the Christian education of adults has been one of the most neglected phases of church work. While increasing attention was being given to the problem of providing more adequate religious instruction for children and youth, adult religious education lagged behind through its failure to capitalize upon new insights regarding the learning process that have emerged from psychological research and the neglect of experimentation in ways of enriching the Christian experience of adults through improved patterns of education.

Much of the retardation of adult religious education has been due to two factors: first, the assumption that adults are so fixed in their habits of thinking and acting that they cannot be changed—"you can't teach an old dog new tricks" was so widely accepted that it seemed almost like heresy to doubt the validity of this dictum when applied to human beings; and, second, the general use of the lecture method in teaching, with an almost complete disregard of the larger possibilities in creative group interaction. But no one who keeps reasonably abreast of the rapidly growing literature in adult Christian education can fail to note that the climate is rapidly changing. Alert leaders now know that adults can learn; that most of them, particularly young adults, want to learn if they are given the opportunity under circumstances that encourage their responsible participation; and that some methods of teaching are more productive of desirable growth than others.

Professor John McKinley, the author of the present volume, is well qualified to open new vistas in the expanding horizons of adult religious education. As a teacher of adult education in one of our leading universities, he has kept in touch with the results of research and experimentation in the general field. And as one of the leaders in the "Indiana Plan of Adult Religious Education," he has pioneered in the application of the new knowledge to the special needs of Christian education.

His book successfully spans the chasm between the behavioral sciences and the practical work of the churches. Without parading his knowledge of psychology, group processes, and the principles of personality development, he nevertheless uses this knowledge expertly in dealing with the problems of methodology. This should prove of great value to church workers who are not conversant with the literature of research but feel the need of utilizing these results in the improvement of their teaching methods. Professor McKinley's treatment is practical and phrased in simple language, but it is based upon the dependable findings of research and experimentation and is presented in a way that directly serves the needs of workers in the local church who must carry on their work without specialized training.

Professor McKinley rightly regards method as a means of arranging opportunities for learning, of providing relationships that will enhance the possibilities of growth; and he relates method to the needs and capacities of experiencing persons. He denies that method can be properly regarded as a "gimmick" or a bag of tricks which can be utilized without respect to the requirements of an effective teaching-learning situation.

Appropriately, he begins his study with a consideration of the nature of the adult learner—his uniqueness, egocenteredness, sensitivity to threats, polarity between dependence and independence, emotionality, and resistance to change. He discusses the significance of these elements in the makeup of a typical adult and considers their implications for education. He then describes most helpfully the conditions that lead to effective participation in a learning experience. His chapter on motivation, though brief and compact, shows clearly the importance of motives in any effective plan for the improvement of teaching procedures. It is difficult to see how this complicated problem could be dealt with more constructively within such a limited space.

Against the background of an understanding of the nature of persons, teaching method is presented as a way of enlisting and guiding persons in the pursuit of their own growth and learning. A number of creative methods are described in sufficient detail to enable the inexperienced leader to grasp both the rationale underlying their use and the manner of their operation. Illustrations are offered of how each method can be applied to church school situations varying from 45 minutes to an hour and a half. In each case, "desirable conditions" are outlined in such a way as to facilitate planning; and the "dangers" are pointed out so that the principal pitfalls may be avoided. The book, therefore, is more than just a "how to do it yourself" manual; it is a useful guide toward responsible and creative group activity.

Books on educational method are often defective in one or the other of two directions. On the one hand, they may be so highly "theoretical" that they are of little practical help to one who must deal with the problems of an actual classroom situation. Or they may be so "practical" that little assistance is offered toward gaining a fundamental understanding of the nature and significance of the task in which the teacher-leader is engaged. This book is an admirable example of how the two interests may be combined in a single presentation.

The thoughtful reader will recognize that this brief book cannot possibly provide the basis for an *adequate* understanding of the theory and practice of creative teaching with adults. But he will find that it is an excellent introduction and a dependable guide. Teachers of adults will find many occasions to consult its pages for help in setting up and using the methods outlined.

LAWRENCE C. LITTLE, Chairman
Department of Religious Education
University of Pittsburgh

PART 1.

Motives

Chapter 1

The Nature of
the Adult Learner

Christian education activities are vehicles of Christian experience. These experiences should help us understand and improve our relationship with God, with ourselves, and with each other so that we may serve him better. Group methods are tools we can use to help organize learning experiences toward these ends.

Somehow the wisdom of teachers, the Christian teachings, and the experience and obstacles of learners must be brought into relationship in the teaching-learning experience. The difficulty is that methods alone only provide opportunities; they do not guarantee that persons will use the opportunities. The "gimmick" user often seizes upon new methods, expecting them to provide not only an operational procedure but also the necessary emotional conditions that are equally important *but not inherent in the methods.* He forgets that method alone is not the answer. Persons are prior to methods, and the methods we use must be appropriate to their problems and needs.

Although effective teachers or leaders of adults must know various methods and how they can be used, it is equally important that they know something about the nature of adults as learners—what motivates them, what conditions underlie their effective participation, and what conditions help promote the acceptance of personal responsibility for learning.

Certain adult characteristics are significant to the educator. They are used here to describe adults and why they react as they do in learning programs. Some of these characteristics which we all share are advantageous to the educator; none of them is inherently "bad" or "good." They just help describe how we are—our nature—and they should be considered in planning adult Christian-education programs.

We are each unique

Each of us has a different background of life experiences and thus a different framework in which to organize and understand experience. Although we have *similar* problems, needs, and experiences, and even though these samenesses make it possible for us to learn together, it is a basic fact that we each differ. This is of fundamental importance to the Christian adult educator for two reasons. First it means that we each bring something different to the learning experience and can each make a potentially different contribution to it. Second it means that we each have individual problems and needs that are slightly different from those of others and must be ministered to during the learning experience. We do not sacrifice a few persons for the sake of many. Tasks are less important than persons (remember the story of the one lost sheep). The Christian learning group can avoid the goal-trap of covering a given amount of material in a given time. Persons, not materials, should be at the center. Our uniqueness warns against rigorous standardization and impersonality in the learning activity.

The background of unique experiences we each have is one of the chief assets we can put to use. We learn in terms of what we know or think we know from experience; so it is vital that we tap learners' experiences whenever possible. The mechanics of how we go about this is a problem of method; when and to what degree depend upon the learners, the subject, and the goals of the meeting.

We are ego-centered

Self-respect and feelings of personal adequacy and worth are absolutely essential, but we often tend to think of ourselves as the center of the universe. Excessive self-centeredness in a Christian learning group can defeat the basic purpose of the activity because it can prevent us from relating to others and to God as parts of the same corporate body. Teachers and learners in Christian groups are charged with helping each other meet individual needs. This means that we must try to *understand* the feelings of our colearners, *not judge* them. We cannot "put ourselves in others' shoes" if our pride drives us to *insist* that our opinion is the right one, that his opinion is a wrong one. Prideful contention by competitive learners and unbending defenders of the texts do untold damage. Most of us are oriented to competition, and we tend to get something for ourselves. Certainly, we like to be right; but labelling someone "right" and someone "wrong" is not as important as finding out *why* persons feel as they do and the significance of those feelings.

We are fearful

Most of us feel threatened and insecure when faced by the unknown. First of all we fear people—our teachers and colearners, people we do not *really* know. We fear to reveal our ignorance to them, particularly to teachers. We fear we will mispronounce words or use bad grammar, and we often fear to admit our true feelings and our doubts even to ourselves, since we all are engaged in maintaining a self-image of competence.

What we fear, or at least seek to avoid, in group situations is not just persons but their disapproval. We fear our performance will not match the standard of behavior which "they" set. This points to one of man's basic needs: acceptance as he is. A theologian once said that the gospel could be expressed in three words: *you are accepted* (not acceptable).

Fear often causes learners to withhold contributions, to refrain from asking for clarification, to hide individual learning problems and needs, and sometimes to stay at home.

Introducing new educational methods to church groups is in a sense creating a situation that represents the unknown or the unfamiliar. Some fear is usually involved, both on the part of the teacher-leader and the learners. The teacher-leader risks the disapproval of the learners and the learners fear they will be revealed as personally lacking in their new roles. These fears are minimized in adult groups in which (1) the teacher-leader is recognized as a learner too, both by himself and by the members, and (2) the group members know each other fairly well, have developed freedom of expression, and have experienced acceptance of each other through active participation in a learning activity.

We have a dual nature

We are caught in a dilemma because we are pulled in two directions by conflicting needs. We each seek dependence and we each seek independence. On the one hand, each of us is a unique person who wishes to express his individual differences and assert himself in his own way. This is a natural urge. On the other hand, no man is an island, for we depend upon each other's support and acceptance in order to preserve our well-being. Perhaps nowhere is this conflict so significant as in a Christian learning group, where, above all places, we should expect to be accepted as a child of God. But this basic conflict is never entirely resolved. When a learner expresses an idea or feeling obviously different from those of the group he inevitably experiences feelings of guilt. Eventually he usually tries to fit into the group on some basis at the expense of his true feelings. This, too, is frustrating and builds back toward expression of independence. So are we shuttled back and forth in this state of *ambivalence:* contradictory feelings with respect to the same situation. Some of us are predominantly dependent, preferring to stifle our individuality and not risk the possible disapproval of our colearners. This means we do not present our true selves and do not creatively wrestle with our learning problems. Instead we spend our time outwardly agreeing against our will (denying our experience) or forcibly keeping silent. Others of us tend to be too independent; we spend much time asserting our differences and little time examining and honestly trying to understand other points of view. Both the overly dependent and the overly independent person are insecure. One denies his own experience; the other denies the experience of others.

We are emotional beings

Two commonly accepted ideas—both erroneous—are responsible for much malpractice in adult Christian education. Both of them overlook the essentially emotional nature of the learner. One idea is that an educational activity is one in which learners should listen and absorb facts to be applied later; and the second idea is that getting people into an argument will produce creative learning. Both of these ideas assume that man is basically rational; that listening or arguing starts rational processes that will lead persons to change their attitudes and behaviors in desirable ways. But most of us are neither emotionally mature nor basically rational. We need more than information or a logical demonstration of the inadequacy of our opinions. We do not automatically discard our cherished ideas in the face of facts: non-Christian attitudes and behaviors do *not* result from our ignorance of the facts, but rather from our emotional inability to accept and act on them. We must be prepared emotionally to accept facts and to work together in conflict. Methods and techniques cannot do this job for us, but they can provide opportunities for us to learn how to do it.

We resist change

Fundamentally the human organism resists change. Each of us is a "self" made up of traits, attitudes, and behaviors which we have organized in such a way that we are fairly comfortable and adjusted to life situations. We try to stay in this comfortable state of equilibrium, and we fight against anything that threatens to change this "workable" organization of "self." An effective Christian education program, however, is deliberately designed to help us change, and thus it is a threat to us. We are continually faced with "oughts" and "shoulds" of Christian living, by what Christ has said and done, as our supreme example. So we tend to protect ourself against recognizing our personal need to change.

Our usual defenses against change are fairly well defined. Let us trace a typical cycle of resistance in a Christian learning group and describe common defense mechanisms you will encounter:

> 1. Some person or text presents a way we ought to behave as Christians (or someone states an opinion or belief).

> 2. The behavior or belief or opinion is different from, or opposed to, how we behave or believe. A conflict arises within us: our present organization of self *versus* a new element. Either to understand or to accept the new means we must reorganize our present self.

> 3. We avoid this conflict *within* us. We defend ourself against possible change in order to stay as we are, and assimilating different points of view is a form of change. We have several ways we tend to flee from our *inner* learning struggle:

>> a) We can attack, *outwardly,* some*body* or some*thing* by attempting to prove that a person or a printed passage is wrong. Thus a discussion may become an *inter*personal conflict between persons to avoid the necessary *intra*personal learning struggle. We can flee not only into

argument, but into intellectual realms, into triviality, into procedural haggling, and so forth.

b) We can withdraw physically. This can take the form of a drop in attendance or refusal to participate vocally in the activity—silence.

c) We can withdraw mentally by not trying honestly to understand the new viewpoint, by not *really* listening. Some people call this security measure "selective inattention." We tend to hear what we want to hear.

d) We can rationalize by developing a set of plausible but unsound reasons that justify our present organization of self.

e) We can project ourself as we now are. This usually takes the form of reasserting our present position or modifying the new idea so that it fits in with our established position.

The effective teacher recognizes that resistance is neither bad nor good, but an educational fact. Our methods must take account of this fact. We learners change ourselves productively when we struggle with our inner conflicts, not against each other or a teacher. This points to certain educational needs:

1. Opportunities to express our differences.

2. Recognition by learners that resistance is natural.

3. Willingness to help each other struggle internally with our learning problems.

4. Mutual trust among colearners, which frees us from defending ourself as we now are.

Chapter 2

Conditions of
Effective Participation

Gimmicks will not sustain active participation over a period of time. The key to getting active participation lies in getting participants to accept a personal share of responsibility for the success of the learning venture. They tend to accept this responsibility most readily when they become personally involved in the learning program. And they are most likely to become personally involved when certain conditions exist. The purpose of this section is to describe briefly some of the most significant conditions that support and encourage creative[1] participation by adults. Practices useful in developing these conditions are suggested in some cases. Alternative practices are cited occasionally since the teacher-leader will sometimes be operating on a 40-minute schedule and at other times will have an hour or more. In any case, the developing of these conditions undergirds the most successful use of the group methods described later in this booklet.

---

[1]Creative in two senses: (1) in the sense that the learners' motives are inherent in the educational activity itself and (2) in the sense that learners themselves make discoveries that lead toward growth.

Shared planning and evaluation

One of the great problems of education is to help learners feel responsible for the success of the learning activity. The only practical way to bring this about is to help them take a responsible share in planning and evaluating the activity. Continued sharing of these two functions over a period of time will lead participants to accept personal responsibility for the outcome of the activity. The successful shift of responsibility from teacher-leader to participants is highly desirable since it signals personal involvement, which further motivates advance preparation for learning and increased participation.

The group or class members can share in selecting topics, setting goals, and choosing informational resources and group methods. If the class is too large to make these decisions as a body, a committee of five to 10 persons can assist the teacher-leader in making these decisions between meetings. In cases in which the topic or subject is dictated by a quarterly, participants can indicate a week in advance which problems or emphases they wish to consider. This can be done at the close of each session or in between-session planning meetings. There is no short cut to improving our learning programs. Experts cannot do our job for us.

Shared goals are necessary if the group is to work toward the same educational end and evaluate their efforts. Goals should be specific, attainable, visible to the group if possible, and stated in terms of what *learners can* do (not what teachers *will* do), for example, "to identify our obstacles to personal prayer," "to find ways of overcoming our obstacles to personal prayer," "to overcome our obstacles to personal prayer." The first two of these goals, you will note, help define what will happen *during* the meeting; the latter one is a desirable outcome that may *result from* the meeting. Shared goal-setting helps participants commit themselves to, and give direction to, the learning activity. The significance of shared oral evaluation cannot be overemphasized. If we are to improve our learning programs, we must first identify the strong and weak points in them and then see how they can be better conducted. It is not a matter of introducing evaluation, since that takes place anyway—usually in cars as participants go home or on the front steps of the church. The problem is to organize a 5- or 10-minute evaluation session in which the group participates together regularly.

All participants can share in at least two kinds of informal evaluation: (1) they can help judge how effective the learning process is and how it might be changed (by giving their reactions at the conclusions of the meetings, either orally or by checking items on a prepared slip of paper) and (2) they can share, periodically, what outcomes have resulted from the meetings.

The added significance of shared evaluation and some ways of carrying it on are described in the next section, "Freedom of Expression."

Freedom of expression

Productive freedom of expression is marked by our willingness to deal openly with our real learning problems. It is *not* a license for hair-raising confessionals or scathing attacks on individuals as persons. Freedom develops mainly as we actually experience the feeling of being accepted as we are by our colearners. This experience comes only as learners actively participate together. Freedom is not brought into being by a teacher's proclamation. These are a few conditions and techniques useful in developing freedom:

1. Class or group members need to know each other as individuals. Get-togethers outside of group activities are helpful; so are name tags, coffee hours, and working together on planning committees between meetings.

2. The teacher-leader's example is important. Since he helps set the standard for the group, he must not only encourage freedom verbally but illustrate it by being willing and able to admit his own ignorances and obstacles to understanding.

3. Freedom develops more rapidly if the group members accept the development of freedom openly as a stated goal or desirable condition. If the group is small and meets regularly, it is helpful for them to discuss the nature of the freedom they desire and to identify obstacles they recognize in developing it.

4. Topics that center on the experience of everyday Christian living are potentially productive for developing freedom. Topics that touch common individual needs both contribute to and result from the development of freedom.

5. Shared oral evaluations of each meeting will, over a period of time, help in the development of freedom. This can be done by allotting the last five to 10 minutes of each meeting to an appraisal of how the *entire group* worked together as a team toward a common goal trying to spotlight what helped and what hindered the learning process. Not individuals but the entire group effort is examined *by the participants and the teacher-leader together*. One tech-

nique is to have one participant serve as *observer* during the meeting, and report what he observed at the conclusion. This report serves as a "kick-off" for a five-minute oral evaluation by group members. The observer should have a checklist so that he knows what to look for during the meeting.

His checklist will be something like this: He makes notes on *how* the group works—the forces that appear to be affecting the operation of the group. He does *not* keep a running record of what is said. The observer attempts to answer such questions as:

Was participation balanced?
Was effort directed toward common goals?
How well did we stick to our task?
What seemed to hinder our progress?
How well did we communicate with each other?
Did there appear to be tension in the group?

How well did participants appear to accept joint responsibility for the program?

An alternative way is for the leader-teacher, using a checklist of learning-group characteristics, to lead the group to express itself on each point as he leads the evaluation. For the first several meetings the leader himself usually must offer judgments and elicit comments as he proceeds from point to point on the checklist. The first few evaluations are likely to produce much back-patting and many surface observations, but continuing evaluation over a period of several meetings usually brings about free expression of *how persons feel* about the learning experience and how it could be improved. The expression and acceptance of these feelings signify the developing of freedom.

An educational class or group that meets regularly should spend a meeting, periodically, identifying outcomes of their educational activity—learning how the lives of the participants have been affected or not affected by their participation in it. This kind of evaluation can be depersonalized sufficiently and made less threatening if participants hand in ahead of time brief, unsigned answers to specific evaluative questions. The answers can be organized into categories and used as the subject of the evaluative discussion. One value of this process comes from participants recognizing not only areas of progress but that their colearners are "like me" and have obstacles in common.

Feeling of personal security

It has long been known that what we actually learn is affected to a large extent by how we *feel* about our colearners and about our own self—our adequacy. When participants feel sufficient personal security in a group, they are better able to face the learning talk without worry about appearing ignorant. These feelings of security grow as we find through experience that we can trust our colearners and that we are worthy individuals in their eyes. No gimmicks can develop these feelings; they come as we *experience* acceptance from both our teacher-leaders and our colearners *in the learning activity*. All we can do here is mention a few things that have caused some learners to feel rejected as persons (that is, as unworthy, insignificant, inferior, "second class," unimportant):

℃ when the teacher-leader or the group participants appear not to listen to my contribution.

℄ when nobody responds to my contribution and it is left dangling in embarrassed silence.

℄ when my contribution is not recorded on the board with the others.

℄ when someone seems to dismiss my contribution as not important.

℄ when I think someone is "talking down" to me or treating me condescendingly.

℄ when someone interrupts me to make what he thinks is a more significant contribution.

℄ when other participants whisper or doodle while I'm trying to communicate with them.

℄ when someone attacks me (we must support the person when we disagree with his ideas).

℄ when someone corrects my pronunciation, grammar, and spelling.

Active, voluntary self-expression

We cannot productively force others to become responsible learners or to extend themselves outward in their relationships. Self-discipline and acceptance of personal responsibility for the task of the group must be activated eventually by each person within himself. For this reason we should not attempt to force persons to serve in some capacity or to express themselves. We give them opportunity after opportunity to contribute orally or to volunteer for the planning committee, for an evaluation committee, for the job as moderator or leader or observer or recorder or to handle room arrangements.

A question directed forcefully at a shy person or at someone who does not yet feel at home in the group is likely to make him feel that he is "on a spot." It is usually best to direct questions toward persons you think will not be embarrassed. Once the shy person has ventured a contribution or a significant nod, perhaps he can be safely drawn in further without risk if the group is not too large. Part of a teacher-leader's job is to protect persons from being "volunteered" by others or forced to give an opinion. One familiar malpractice is, "Now we will go around the circle, each one giving his opinion of this question and stating his reasons."

Acceptance of responsibilities by group participants

Certain responsibilities, such as planning and evaluating, we have already mentioned. Yet there are some other responsibilities which learners and teacher-leaders can accept jointly to make the orally participative experience most effective:

1. We should prepare to participate. If we have had a hand in planning the program and feel it is directed to our own problem or need, we are likely to prepare in advance for meetings. This is particularly true if it is plain that the leader won't do it for us and that the other participants will expect us to prepare.

2. We should listen to each other actively, help each other understand what is said, help keep the learning activity related to experience, help keep on the track, prevent domination by a few persons, support each other as persons, and help resolve problem situations that arise during the session. In the participative experience such tasks are traditionally left

to the leader-teacher, but they can be shared by *all* participants (1) if they are made aware that these are shared responsibilities, (2) if they are encouraged to accept these responsibilities, and (3) if some time is given to learning these responsibilities during the group activity and to evaluating the group effort in terms of them.

Appropriate physical arrangements

We often tend to disregard the importance of certain physical factors in a group meeting. Many of us apparently think of them as unimportant or trivial. For example, most meetings could make good use of a blackboard or a chart pad and butcher paper—this basic visual aid is fundamental. We tend to remember best what we receive through various sense organs. Purposes or goals, key words, outlines, group contributions—all these things usually need to be spotlighted at different times during a learning activity.

Tables and movable chairs are also a great asset in many cases. Various methods require different physical arrangements, and these differences are not just a matter of custom. Not that the arranging of chairs, tables, and learners in a certain pattern causes participation magically to become more meaningful. The fact is, the distribution of learners in a given pattern is usually a way of improving communication and indicating physically the responsibilities of the participants in the activity. Thus, in a group discussion we sit roughly in a circle, because we are equally responsible and we must be able to see those to whom we are to speak and listen. In a speech the speaker is normally in front so he can see us and we can see him, yet not be distracted by looking at others' reactions.

A table at the center of a discussion group helps serve as a unifying force and as a psychological support for timid or fearful participants. It serves a similar function for a panel of resource persons who sit in front of a class or an audience.

The size of the meeting room as it relates to the size of the group also tends to affect the quality and quantity of participation. A small group needs a small room; a larger group needs a larger room.

In short the use of certain physical items and arrangements mentioned later are not just the result of crusty convention. Most of them are supported by logical reasons and by research. To overlook them is to risk failing to serve our classes and groups adequately as educational guides.

Chapter 3

Some Notes on
Motivation

Motivation is an essential condition of learning. Anything that helps to activate us or to influence us to do something is a factor in the motivation process. It is useful, however, to think of motivation as an *internal process.* Conditions within the individual are the significant things that cause him to seek particular goals: his interests, desires, and needs as he interprets them. An educator can stimulate a person's interest and help him discover reasons for participating in an activity. But the goals and motives of the learner are his own. Educational situations, therefore, must be created in which learners are able to identify worthy individual goals and motives.

One of the major jobs of an effective adult educator is that of creating opportunities in which people can activate educational goals and motives. This is often called the first step in educational motivation.

Developing situations which stimulate adults to participate in an educational church program can be more than simply making a pulpit announcement or running a blurb in the weekly bulletin. These two methods are useful and should be used. But other kinds of stimulation are often required to get people committed to an educational program. Effective stimulation requires that prospective participants make certain key recognitions. If potential participants can make these recognitions, the chances of their attending and participating in a proposed program will be maximized.

Four key recognitions

1. Recognition of a personal problem that might be solved by attendance at and participation in the proposed program. By a problem we mean a difficulty—some obstacle to harmonious Christian living. A personal problem is not necessarily a deep, horrifying predicament. It is any difficulty with which we can personally identify ourself. For some reason we tend to resist problem-recognition in terms of something that exists. We are more prone to identify a problem as being the lack of something that is needed. Thus people often tend to recognize problems indirectly in terms of needs. If we can devise situations in which persons can make a personal problem recognition, as well as a need recognition, then the stimulation to participate is increased.

2. Recognition of a personal need (lack) that could be met by participation. We must expect people to recognize superficial needs at the outset. As a matter of fact, they are accustomed to recognizing needs in terms of subject-matter information, which is only a means of overcoming personal deficiencies of Christian living. In one sense certain information *is* a need. But more realistic needs center about our lacks or deficiencies of God-centered living. Situations in which we can recognize some of our needs in terms of personal everyday living are effective in stimulating future attendance and participa-

tion. It must be held in mind that we resist recognizing our needs openly in personal terms, much less in *specific* personal terms. For this reason the outward expressions of needs (and of problems for that matter) are likely to be impersonal and general. But even these expressions are a basis for activating the educational process of discovery in which we can learn to recognize more of our real problems and needs.

3. Anticipation of achieving personally satisfying outcomes within a reasonable length of time in the proposed program.

4. Recognition that colearners will have problems and/or needs similar to ours.

One of the most effective ways to help persons achieve some of these recognitions is through a planned program in which the potential participants (1) meet as a group,[1] and (2) discover and voice the recognitions themselves. The group setting is invaluable since it provides an opportunity for shared recognitions, ego-involvement, and witnessed commitment to the future program. When members of a group recognize shared feelings, anxiety tends to be reduced and a positive force is set in motion.

Devising group situations in which participants can discover and express in some form recognition #1 and/or #2 is indeed difficult. Yet these two recognitions must be made first; #3 and #4 depend upon the first two. Logical, intellectual presentations in which somebody "proves" the existence of certain problems or needs may stimulate us, but often will not move us to make the recognitions and do something about them. By and large we are not moved by someone else's set of facts. We must make

[1] It is often done effectively through personal contacts of individuals. I know of no "magical" ways to get people involved.

our own recognitions emotionally as well as intellectually if we are to act on them. And we are more likely to accept something we discover ourselves, since we tend to identify ourselves with it emotionally.

Program strategies

To plan meetings in which participants will become motivated to attend future meetings, we need to have some kind of strategy to guide us. One major strategy is to plan meetings which aim at meeting some needs—a straight educational meeting. There is no good substitute for this approach over the long haul. A sound creative program will eventually draw in more and more people. Another strategy, however, is to plan a meeting (or preferably a series of meetings) designed primarily to arouse interest and bring about the participant recognitions mentioned above. This type of program may be educational in the sense that information is presented in some subject area, but its main purpose is to open vistas of program opportunities and to get participants committed to a future program.

It is possible to look at the latter type of strategy as having four phases; these phases do not necessarily follow in a fixed order:

1. **Stimulus.** Usually this is a presentation of some sort which gives information and arouses interest. It can be a problem/need area objectified in a film or in a role play. Or it can be a speech, a panel presentation, etc., used to focus attention on some problem/need area. Sometimes it takes the form of a written or oral report summarizing some present situation. It can be some interest-arousing information given in

a problem/need area. It can also be a program-proposal stated outright.

2. **Identification of Problems/Needs.** This is often a small-group process in which the participants take part after a "stimulus" presentation in order to formulate questions or reactions. This activity can also *precede* the stimulus phase and in fact become a sort of stimulus. In some extended-program formats, the participants' identification of the problems/needs in their own terms is a multisession process that is given much emphasis. The tension between "what is" and "what ought to be" can be highlighted by interposing several short *stimulus* situations (mentioned above) at appropriate times.

3. **Recognition by Participants of Problems/Needs Held in Common.** This recognition is something that we hope will take place within and among the participants. Two factors often help promote the shared recognitions: (1) the interaction in the small-group identification process mentioned above, and (2) making visible to all participants the results of the small-group operation by means of a blackboard or the use of crayon and butcher paper. This phase takes place usually during the forum activity in which the small-group reactions are discussed. The "forum period" may be devoted to analyzing the results of the small groups to see whether they think a series of meetings would be helpful. Sometimes a resource person gives some short answers to small-group questions then indicates the need for an extended program in which they can deal more adequately with these questions. Leaders who perceive a pattern of common prob-

lems/needs expressed should take every opportunity to point out the possibility of dealing with them in the proposed program.

4. Commitment to Program. Some program planners find it advantageous to get some kind of visible commitment from persons who would be willing to participate in future meetings. A show of hands or the signing of a sheet of paper are two methods commonly used. Checking a "yes" or "no" on a post-meeting evaluation sheet is frequently used. But this private method of indicating interest in future attendance offers no clues publicly as to *who* and *how many* seem interested in attending. To some potential participants a knowledge of who and how many is important. This kind of commitment, secured in haste at the conclusion of a meeting, is not the real thing. The real thing must be demonstrated over a period of time through participation in the program itself.

Although the four phases described in general terms above can be telescoped into one short meeting, they are likely to be more effective in a one- or two-day series of meetings. The search for short-term magical motivation opportunities involving large numbers of persons is slowly giving way to the use of longer-term programs which involve smaller groups of persons with more intensity.

There are some problem/need areas in which adults tend to be more highly motivated than in others. The general rule might be stated something like this: the best opportunities for bringing about educational change lie in problem areas in which we want to improve and in which the people around us wish or expect us to do better.

Two of these areas that are best known are (1) filling the role of parent satisfactorily and (2) being successful in our job or work (where we make our living). Christianity speaks clearly to both these tasks. In other words, church programs for adults that are beamed at problems and needs in these two areas stand a good chance of drawing participants—particularly persons who range in age from their twenties to their late forties. (Please hold in mind that we are talking here about programs that take advantage of the immediate interest and readiness of adults.)

Studies indicate that generally speaking many of us become less interested in vocational advancement in our late forties. By this time we begin to see our limits, to experience bodily changes, and to see our time as becoming limited. We stop asking so many "how" questions and begin asking some "what" and "why" questions about life and religion and our role in both. Several adult educators have said that persons in the middle years are the persons who most easily become educationally motivated. It is well, however, to remember that high individual motivation for certain kinds of activities does not depend exclusively upon age. For example, no matter how old we are, whenever we become parents, new church members, parents of children beginning to attend church school, or persons eligible for retirement, we are likely to be most receptive to certain kinds of programs—those that promise to deal with problems and needs that concern us at that time. Church adult educators should take these factors into consideration when they plan programs. Knowing the local situation and the people in it is a necessity for good planning. Theory and general principles are of little more than academic value unless they are used to gain insight into the specific, unique local setting. In the final analysis the local program must be shaped by the problems and needs of the persons involved.

Some Basic Principles

At least five basic principles undergird the motivation process in educational activities. These principles you will recognize as inherent in the procedures and conditions outlined in Chapters 1 and 2. They are outlined here as touchstones to refer to when organizing either formal teaching situations or more informal group-centered activities.

1. **Intentional learning.** The teacher must somehow convey to participants the idea that they are expected to learn. This is a low-keyed motivation procedure. We tend to try to do what we think others expect of us, within certain limits. With adults we must not insist that they *must* learn, nor should we tell them *what* they must learn. If the group is not too large, it is well to have the learners frame goals they can all agree on. Goals make intention specific.

2. **Standard of expected achievement.** Coupled closely with intention is the use of some standard of expected achievement. This standard of expected achievement can take the form of hoped-for desirable outcomes so long as these are seen as attainable, concrete, and presented as possible, not insisted upon, outcomes. This standard is, of course, most binding and valuable if it takes the form of group goals created by the learners themselves. A group standard tends to be more effective and acceptable than a teacher's. Learners need to be supported in their

anticipated change by others who "are like me" and who "are trying to change as I am." The teacher-leader is a key standard setter. If he is teaching freedom of expression, teamwork, and acceptance, he must himself provide an example of these qualities in action.

3. **Knowledge of progress and results.** In the public schools it is more easy to invoke the principle of feeding back to the learner some knowledge of his progess. Teachers can do so because they are the ones who set the goals, and because progress can be symbolized by grades, which can be compared. In adult Christian education we do not work for grades or for verbal learning which can be parroted back on examination papers. Only the learner can really activate this important principle. The teacher can, of course, encourage the class or group on the process level by citing improved participation, preparation, teamwork, and willingness to wrestle with learning problems. At its best, however, this principle should lead us periodically to provide some time for participants to compare notes on how they are faring in putting their Christian learning to work.

Appraising our "progress and results" in a group setting has some disadvantages, since there are many private occurrences we have no business talking about. There is some basis for a sharing of appraisals, however, if the members themselves have set specific shared goals at the beginning of a series of meetings. There must be some freedom and trust among the class or group members if this important motivational principle is to be used effectively. For remarks about achieving freedom, see "Freedom of Expression" in Chapter 2.

4. **Interest.** We are most likely to learn when we like the learning activity. For this reason we would do well to organize the activity around elements in which interest inheres. We cannot always reconcile interests with needs, but the fact remains that interests point toward needs, and one task of Christian education is to help us learn how to discover our needs.

We sometimes confuse *interests* with *needs*. An interest is usually thought of as "a liking for" *a given activity*. Needs are lacks or deficiencies we have or feel we have. We seek activities through which we can satisfy the needs we feel.

If we ask ourself why we are interested in a certain activity, we are pushing one step deeper to find what need motivates that interest. Interests point back to needs because an interest is the expression of some kind of need we feel. Interests are often readily identifiable by educators because their signs are apparent. The needs which are symbolized by an interest are not always so apparent. For example, we cannot assume that our interests *(our liking for an activity)* and our needs (lacks) are both directly related to the subject of a meeting. We may attend a meeting on "sewage disposal," not because the *subject* is vital to us but because (a) we are lonely, or because (b) it is an opportunity for us to show off some knowledge publicly. In neither case would the subject of the meeting be directly related to our need (a) companionship or (b) ego-satisfaction in this case.

Our interest (liking for the activity) would be apparent. Our needs would be remote indeed from "sewage disposal."

This is not to say that all needs should be met at the subject-matter level. Many an adult has come away from a church meeting with a renewed feeling of relationship with God and God's family, but without any new understanding of the topic that was studied. For these persons the "content" of the meeting (the cognitive meanings and understandings they took home) had little to do with the stated subject of the meeting.

5. **Ego-involvement.** The learning experience is most effective when it has personal meaning for the learners. When we identify our *self* with the success of the learning activity we are involved emotionally in it. This involvement can be at the content level (as a result of dealing with a subject with personal meaning); or it can be at the process level (when we feel responsible for the way the meeting is carried on or for helping other learners). At its best the involvement should be at both levels. This condition points out the need of giving learners a responsible share in developing and conducting their learning activities.

Ego-involvement is wrongly used in Christian education when it is employed deliberately to foster competition or to make learners feel that their worth as persons depends upon their performance or success in the learning activity. It is always dangerous to separate means and ends in Christian education.

6. Identification - want to be like him for what he is. Paul - " Follow me as I follow Christ."

PART 2.

Methods

Chapter 4

The Expanding Panel

The expanding panel is a combination of presentation and discussion. Best used with groups of 20 to 40 persons, it is an informal type of program which can be adapted to a 45-minute situation or extended to an hour or an hour and a half. The program has two basic parts:

℃ a 15- to 30-minute exploratory discussion of a given topic presented by a panel of six to 12 persons who are

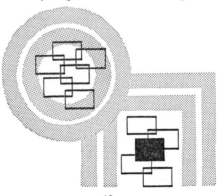

closely surrounded on three sides by the audience, followed by

⟨ a physical rearrangement of *all participants* into one large circle in which the entire group continues the discussion for an additional 30 minutes to one hour. The panel is the nucleus that activates the situation; then it literally expands and loses its identity in the total forum group.

A Program Pattern

Two time-scheme examples of an expanding panel program are given below. The first illustrates the use of this method during an hour and a half meeting. The second example illustrates how this method can be adapted to a 45-minute adult-class period.

7:30 P.M.   Prayer
             Chairman of meeting or leader of discussion panel briefly describes the task and procedures of the entire meeting; introduces the topic; encourages audience to jot down notes and prepare to participate; introduces the panel, and leads in informal discussion.

8:00 P.M.   Leader stops discussion
             Panel and audience push back their chairs into one large circle.
             Leader asks group at which point they wish to continue the discussion, or for disagreements, or for questions that need to be raised. If information is needed, a resource person may be used. Forum discussion continues.

8:40 to
8:50   Summary, conclusion, prayer.

If this method is adapted to a 45-minute class in which a definite weekly lesson is assigned in a quarterly, the members of the panel have an excellent opportunity to focus on the significance of the lesson in daily Christian living. This usually requires the panel members to meet once during the week to organize (but not rehearse) their discussion. Remember that the panel presents not a series of short speeches, but an organized "bull session" in which the members help each other. It is important to remember that whatever the panel does tends to set the pace for the forum that follows.

9:30 A.M.   Leader of panel briefly describes the task and procedure of the class meeting and the audience responsibilities; may *very* briefly review the lesson; starts the discussion.

9:45   Panel and audience become one forum circle and continue the discussion.

10:00   Summary and evaluation of the process. Volunteer panel members and leader sought for the next session.

10:15   Dismiss.

Values

1. The expanding panel can be adapted to adult church school classes.

2. It can help promote freedom of expression and discussion teamwork on a fairly large scale, depending upon the nature of the topic and the performance of the panel which initiates discussion.

3. It recognizes the need for active-participation-type programs.

4. It can help arouse interest in participating in other adult programs of a more intensive nature.

5. It provides an informal means by which a relatively large group of persons can come to grips with topics of mutual concern.

Desirable Conditions

1. Certain physical conditions are necessary for best results:

> a) A table for the panel on the same level with the audience, which should be seated informally around three sides of the panel.
>
> b) Enough space so that everyone present can sit in one large informal circle during the forum. Try to get eye contact among a maximum of those involved.
>
> c) A blackboard, or easel and butcher paper, on which can be written the topic and a brief discussion outline and goals for the inner group.
>
> d) Movable chairs.

To save time the physical set-up can be arranged prior to the time the class or group is to meet.

2. For best results, the group that initiates discussion should be composed of lay persons who are members of the class or group. It is better yet if they are experienced in discussion teamwork. Their 15- to 30-minute discussion should display freedom of expression and co-operative helpfulness in communicating with each other. The fact that they are lay persons who are willing to give their opinions and to raise problems of personal understanding in a frank

manner can be a powerful means of setting a standard for the whole group.

3. If possible, the class or group should know in advance the nature of what will take place. They should be reminded of their responsibilities at the start of the meeting.

4. The best topics seem to be those which are most relevant to everyday Christian living or understanding. The audience must be able to identify with the problem or need reflected in the topic.

5. A resource person such as a minister or teacher can be very helpful. He should be called upon when facts are needed but he should not seize upon each question as an opportunity to present a sermonette; this will result in a type of authority-dependency in which discussion is reduced to a series of rapid-fire questions directed to the resource person. He then tends no longer to serve the learning process, but to transmit *his* learning to them. He is not to withhold facts, but he must let the participants establish the personal significance of the facts.

6. It is usually advantageous if the leader of the larger forum is a lay person since the resource person can then serve in his proper role and does not have to worry about co-ordinating the process of interaction. Some premeeting planning by the leader of the forum is helpful since he should have a fund of questions he can use to keep the forum purposeful. He should not, however, let his questions determine the progress of the forum if he can get the participants to do so.

7. During the forum the members of the discussion panel (who occupy seats in various spots around the

group circle) should not dominate the conversation. They can serve best by helping draw out others and by promoting (by example) spontaneous contributions, thus accepting certain helpful leadership functions while taking part as group participants.

Dangers

1. The first time or two this process is used, forum participation by audience members will tend to take the form of questions directed to the leader or to the resource person. This is natural and to be expected. And the larger the group the more formal and forum-question-centered it will be. At least three means can be used to help deformalize it over a period of time: (a) the good examples of free discussion set by the panelists, (b) an observer's report at the end of the meeting, in which possible causes and effects of formality are spotlighted, and (c) a visible set of suggested goals and desirable learning conditions printed in large letters and spotlighted at the beginning and at the end of the meeting.

Members of the inner panel should be especially watchful to avoid appearing like special lay theologians. Their purpose is *not* to teach the audience some answers in the topic or subject area. Their main purpose is to open up the topic area by revealing some of their opinions and learning problems in that area. Not lessons or texts, but the *significance* of lessons and texts should be discussed by both the inner panel and the forum group.

3. Do not assume that you can leave the inner panel intact in the center and always get active forum participation. It is best to destroy physically the

identity of the panel in order (a) to avoid the possibility of intergroup competition, (b) to promote face-to-face forum discussion, (c) to free lay members of the inner panel from feeling that they have been thrust into the role of expert.

4. The forum moderator should seek voluntary participation and not involve anyone in a direct question that might cause embarrassment. Nor should he proceed around the circle in an attempt to force each person to make a contribution.

5. The teacher-leader who serves as resource person will probably find himself sorely tempted to fill the silences that may occur during the forum discussion periods the first few times this process is used. These seemingly awkward spots are natural, however, if the group involved has in the past depended almost entirely on a leader to direct them.

It is true that the leader will not always know when information is needed from the resource person, and sometimes he must offer information unsolicited. But if he turns the forum discussion into a traditional teacher-pupil situation, he will find himself, not the participants, thrust back into the role of being responsible for the success of the meeting.

Chapter 5

The Sermon Forum

The sermon forum is given separate treatment here because usually it is applied to a large number of the adults in the congregation; also because special problems are involved in conducting it.

Normally the sermon forum is a 15- to 30-minute sermon followed by active oral participation of the audience. The purpose of this participation is not to criticize the sermon but to explore and assimilate its significance.

The sermon forum can be adapted to many kinds of situations, but it must be bent to fit the situation at hand. It has been successfully used in these kinds of settings:

1. as an adjunct to midweek evening services;

2. to follow up Sunday midmorning services after which there are no adult church school classes;

3. as a means of letting one or two Sunday morning adults classes follow up the sermon as the subject for their class;

4. as a Sunday night follow-up to the Sunday morning sermon, open to all adults in the congregational family;

5. to supplement special series of teaching sermons at certain seasons.

A Program Pattern

The program pattern usually consists of three distinct parts. The first part may occur on Sunday morning followed by the second and third in the evening. Or all three may take place on Sunday morning or Sunday night:

1. A sermon, usually but not necessarily part of a worship service.

2. A period during which the participants gather in discussion groups of six to 10 persons to frame questions, discuss significance, and clarify meanings.

3. An open forum at which all groups come together, ask their questions, and give the minister an

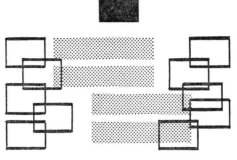

opportunity to help them clarify misunderstandings and applications.

Here is a sample program outline for a Sunday morning sermon forum:

9:30 A.M.   Services, including sermon.
10:15   Adults go to designated rooms or places in groups of six or eight (each with tables and blackboard) where they discuss relevance of sermon and form questions.

10:50   All adults gather in basement for open
               forum; each group asks its questions and
               minister responds.
11:15 to
11:30   Summary and conclusions.

This time schedule would not be appropriate in all
cases. Many churches would have to adapt this approach
wholly to evening services or perhaps use the Sunday
morning sermon as a springboard for a Sunday evening
educational program as in the following instance:

7:30 P.M.   Chairman or minister reminds participants
               that their task is to (a) get a recorder, (b)
               discuss the relevance of the Sunday morning
               sermon, (c) identify obstacles to understand-
               ing the sermon, (d) identify questions on
               applying it. An outline of the sermon is given
               to those who have lost their previous copy.
               Groups go to designated places.
8:15   Participants come together as one group;
               each group reports and asks its questions in
               turn; minister responds to questions in open
               forum.
9:00   Summary, closing prayer.

Values

1. The sermon becomes a more significant educational medium, since the forum provides opportunity for learners actively to assimilate its content in
terms of their personal framework of understanding.

2. Participants are given an opportunity to assume
an active responsibility rather than a passive role in
the teaching-learning process.

3. New adult members of the congregation can be rapidly integrated into the congregational family while it operates as a learning team.

4. The forum provides a concrete example of the congregational family working together actively as a family in educational activities.

5. The questions can provide the minister with valuable information:

a) How effectively he is communicating and areas in which he can improve his effectiveness.

b) What specific points need re-emphasizing in future sermons or other learning activities. Clues to common educational needs emerge through the patterns of questions that are developed in the small groups.

6. This type of forum can lead to increased readiness for more intensive adult programs involving active participation and dealing with individual needs.

Desirable Conditions

Ministers and congregational leaders who wish to adapt this approach to their unique church situations should reflect on these general recommendations:

1. In the small-group phase, from six to 10 persons seem to operate most effectively. Planners must devise some locally acceptable principle for dividing the participants into groups at the first session with a minimum of lost motion. Voluntary friendship groups, age groups (roughly speaking), and the "numbering off" technique have all been used. The composition of the discussion groups begins to stabilize the second

and third times this process is used with a random group.

2. The small discussion groups, in most cases, should not meet in the nave of the church. Walking to another place after the sermon provides a needed "stretch." Also, the nave is not always an ideal place to establish an oral participation tradition. The open forum, on the other hand, *can* be successful in the nave, or church proper, partly because the precedent for frank questioning is established elsewhere in the small groups. The forum portion of the program is usually more successful the first few meetings (a) if it is held in the church basement, the parish house, a large classroom, or the educational building, and (b) if the minister encourages forum participation.

3. Furnishing pencil and paper to participants before the sermon is a good procedure, especially if the minister reminds them that he will not be embarrassed if they take notes while he is speaking.

4. Name cards on the discussion tables relieve people of some of the embarrassment of forgetting names between sessions; they also help fix the association of names with faces for new people in the congregation.

5. The minister is a key figure in the successful use of this approach. He should be informal enough so as not to inhibit participation and should encourage the participants. Four useful techniques have been used:

a) The sermon may be outlined on a blackboard. This serves during the sermon as a visual guide and as a means of seating the group physically close together (within reading range) which is an important, but nonverbal, way of teaching the corporateness of God's family.

b) Introducing each sermon with a few remarks pointing out *the possible general significance* of what he will say gives the participants a listening responsibility and a listening guide.

c) The minister may give "listening cues" during the sermon at important points, for example, "You may want to discuss this point in your groups."

d) A mimeographed outline of the sermon has proved helpful. Usually it is handed out at the conclusion of the sermon.

6. If discussion leaders are appointed ahead of time, it should be made clear that the small-group leaders are not to be teachers or special lay theologians. The minister should openly describe their purpose and function at the start of the program, when he explains the mechanics of the program. Discussion leaders should explain to their groups that they are not resource leaders, or teachers, in the popular sense. Some practitioners prefer not to use preappointed leaders, but voluntary recorders instead, in the small groups.

7. If discussion leaders are used, it is important that they know the purpose of this kind of discussion: (a) to identify some questions or areas needing clarification (groups tend to work more purposefully if they have a specific task), (b) to discuss major points briefly as their significance relates to everyday living, (c) to encourage co-operative voluntary participation.

8. It is advantageous if discussion leaders have had some training in both discussion participation and discussion leadership. They should, as leaders, avoid the role of teacher, remain neutral, avoid dominating, and try to encourage balanced participation. Questions should be formulated *by the group; but individual questions must not be dismissed by the leader or recorder.*

9. Each discussion group should sit in a face-to-face arrangement, if possible around a table.

10. Participants should have a chance to give their reactions to the sermon-forum process and to offer suggestions for improving it. Periodically, a simple postmeeting reaction form can be handed to each of the participants at the conclusion of the forum.

11. Success with this approach seems to vary in the proportion that the minister (a) has, or is able to establish, rapport with the learners, (b) is willing and able to help them relate the sermon information to their lives, and (c) is willing to admit openly when he has no satistfactory answer to a question.

12. It is a good idea to introduce the sermon forum by first finding out (through questionnaire or brief interviews with classes and organizations) what sermon topics would seem to meet needs recognized by the congregation. This serves to publicize the program, involves the congregation in the planning, and thus gives them a listening responsibility.

Dangers

1. Not all sermon subjects are easily related to experiences of daily Christian living. Small-group discussion of some subjects (*e.g.*, some parts of church

history) is sometimes limited to identifying areas that need clarifying. This process works best with "teaching" sermons as distinguished from "inspirational" and "proclamation" sermons.

2. Some discussion leaders (especially untrained ones) assume the role of teacher. By answering what *he* considers simple questions, this type of leader causes some participants to repress questions that to them are not simple. The participant must find Christian acceptance as he is. He must not feel he is "being used" as a means for letting a discussion leader parade his knowledge. A well-intentioned leader sometimes is driven by his zeal to dismiss "simple" questions or answer them himself and get to what *he* considers more weighty matters.

3. A few ministers prefer to avoid this process, particularly the forum part since it can be threatening. Some ministers reflect this feeling by erroneously interpreting this process as a form of sermon criticism. This is definitely not the purpose of the sermon forum.

4. During the final question-and-answer forum period, it is usually not advantageous for the minister to try to answer questions from all the small groups. In some cases the minister is prone to preach another sermon in order to answer one question. It will be necessary for him to exercise self-control; to recognize that all final complete answers cannot be given in a forum period. It has been found expedient to have a layman serve as moderator during the forum period since this procedure relieves the minister from co-ordinating and directing the process of interaction and permits him to serve in his true role—that of resource person.

Chapter 6

Group Discussion

Many are the forms and practices of group discussion. Here is described one approach to the use of group discussion as a learning method for adult church groups. For our purposes we may define group discussion as the informal, purposeful, co-operative exploration of an agreed-on topic by a group of from six to twenty persons.

Uses

1. This method can be used in adult Bible classes having 40 to 50 minutes of class time available each Sunday.

2. It can be adapted to study groups that meet weekly or biweekly.

3. It can be used by young adult church school classes.

4. Group discussion offers a vehicle for organizing evening study groups.

5. It may be used for conducting church school teacher-training sessions.

Desirable Conditions

1. The size of most effective discussion groups varies from eight to 15 participants. Groups with as many as 20 persons have used this method successfully.

The larger the group, however, the more time is required to develop the freedom of expression and the co-operative attitudes and skills necessary for the most productive use of the method.

2. The participants should sit around a table, if possible, and be arranged so that they are all in eye contact. The table lends some persons psychological support, helps unify the group, and tends to eliminate the "second-row fringe," which is not desirable in group discussion.

3. Either a blackboard or newsprint and crayon are highly desirable. This visual tool helps the participants understand the goals, the topic question, and the brief tentative outline of the discussion; also it is a means of keeping discussion related to the topic. In many cases it is valuable to record contributions of the group.

Procedures

1. The Topics

Not all topics are suitable for group discussion. In general we can say that good topics for group discussion are those which are:

> a) recognized by participants as significant and related to the business of Christian living.
>
> b) stated in the form of a question which cannot be answered either "yes" or "no."
>
> c) narrow enough in scope to encourage focused exploration and to discourage broad abstract generalization.

Two general approaches are used to formulate discussion topics for adult church groups: one states the topic in terms of problems of Christian experience; the other centers on subjects or Christian teachings.

Inexperienced discussion groups tend to choose the latter type of topic statement because it allows participants to discuss Christian ideas intellectually in a fairly abstract, impersonal way. This approach is fairly safe since it does not pose the threat of change in a personal way, nor does it require participants to give as much of themselves to the experience.

Consider which of the following two sets of topics leaves the most room to retreat into impersonal speculation, and which focuses on problems of Christian living:

Subject-centered topics

"What is meant by Christian Love?"

"What did Jesus mean by—the meek shall inherit the earth?"

"What is Christian forgiveness according to ————?"

Experience-centered topics

"When—if ever—are we justified in not turning the other cheek?"

"How can we improve our personal prayer life?"

"How truthful should we be in our daily Christian living?"

Obviously Christian teachings should be brought to bear upon problems of Christian living, and it doesn't really matter which of the two ways the topic is stated *so long as these two elements are brought together*. Often, however, a steady diet of subject-centered topics serves to hamper the development of realistic discussion.

One difficulty in topic selection is recognized if church school classes are expected to derive their topics from a Uniform Lesson. A single lesson usually covers a great deal of ground (for example *ALL* of the Ten Commandments or *ALL* of the Twenty-third Psalm). If the class wishes to get beneath the surface and deal with real learning problems in 45 minutes, it may have to focus on only one portion or one aspect of the lesson, for example, ". . . lead me not into temptation . . ." or ". . . thy rod and thy staff, they comfort me . . .," or "In what respects is the Lord's Prayer a good example of a prayer?" or "What things can we justifiably ask for in our prayers?"

2. Personnel

a) *Teacher or Leader?*

Should a teacher-leader (or some other sub-ject-matter authority) serve as discussion leader? Or, should volunteer lay members of the class or group serve as discussion leaders? Either choice has both advantages and disadvantages. In practice the decision usually depends upon the purpose of group discussion as interpreted by those involved. If discussion is interpreted as a leader-follower teaching method, the expert usually leads. If it is interpreted as a joint learn-ing venture with the leader as a catalytic agent, the way is open for volunteer leadership.

If a teacher or subject expert serves as dis-cussion leader, the group members frequently take a passive role, think of themselves as fol-lowers, and fall back on him for direction. In a sense they force him to take a much too active part in the discussion. The leader also is forced to serve in the dual role of resource expert as well as discussion leader—a difficult task indeed. If the leader is not sensitive to his role as encourager and catalyst, he often tends not to help participants wrestle with *their* learning problems, but will turn the discussion into a series of teaching interludes. Thus he abandons the role of discussion leader—the servant who helps the group go where *they* feel they should go. He dictates (or "suggests" strongly), they follow, and the discussion has really belonged to the leader, not to the group participants. Enlightened teachers do not fall into this trap when they serve as discussion leader.

With volunteer leadership, the teacher or subject expert is free to serve as "resource person" (one called upon for information or opinion when needed). With volunteer leaders, discussion may not proceed smoothly for several sessions because leaders and group members are learning how to become jointly responsible for the discussion. This fumbling is the price that is paid when persons learn to accept responsibility. This kind of learning may be as important as covering subject matter.

b) *Responsibilities*

(1) *Of the Discussion Leader*

The leader is not necessarily one who knows the most about the topic, but one who is responsible for co-ordinating the interaction of the group members.

The discussion leader serves the group by helping them do what they want to do as a group. He draws out participation, remains neutral (expresses no personal opinions) on the topic, and does not attempt to lead the group to his own or some other acceptable conclusion. He must learn to fade into the background when the group members can proceed fruitfully without him. He can win only by losing.

Assuming that a group has chosen a topic one week in advance, a leader would have these kinds of duties to perform:

(a) *Before the Meeting*

i) Make a brief tentative outline consisting of the topic question, one or two suggested goals, and three or four subtopics or questions that seem to be crucial in exploring the topic. Avoid the formal outlining procedures (I, A, 1, 2, B, II, etc.).

ii) Develop some questions which *might* be useful in starting discussion and bringing out various sides of the question.

iii) Read the written resource material that has been suggested as helpful information.

iv) Go to the meeting early and put the three elements of your suggested outline on the blackboard to save time during the meeting.

v) Check physical arrangements (chairs, tables, light, ventilation, chalk, etc.).

(b) *During the Discussion*

i) Give a *very* brief introduction, perhaps suggesting the significance of the topic, and submit the outline to the group for them to adjust.

ii) Allow time for the group to adjust the outline if they feel it is necessary. Remember that this is part of their learning task—as important as discussing the subject, because it affects not only *how* it will be covered, but sometimes *who* will actually take part. At first, the group will be slow to accept this responsibility.

iii) Toss out an appropriate question (if it is necessary) to start discussion.

iv) To keep discussion purposeful

℃ remind the group when they are off the track

℃ draw in a maximum number of participants

℃ rephrase contributions which you feel someone has not understood

℃ make opportunities for various points of view to be heard to encourage minority views

℃ prevent domination

℃ record main points on the board concisely (or help or recorder do so). Remember that learning groups don't have to reach concensus to put ideas on the board; learning groups must make group decisions only when they plan (choose topics, set goals, etc.).

℃ encourage freedom of expression.

(c) *After the Discussion*

i) Summarize the discussion if it would be helpful.

ii) Call for observer's report and brief oral evaluation of the session (optional, see p. 23).

iii) Help the group decide on topic and leader(s) for next session.

iv) Help the group identify appropriate sources of information they can use to prepare for next session.

The leader can be of great service if he encourages the group participants to relate the discussion to their present living experience. The outline, the topic question, and the goals can help point toward this desirable end if they are created to do so.

If the discussion group is fairly large (15 persons or larger), it is often advantageous to have coleaders. Two leaders can serve a group better than one. One usually takes the major responsibility for co-ordinating the process of discussion; the other can serve as blackboard recorder and also help promote communication and understanding among group members when he is able. When volunteer leadership is to be used, persons accept the role of leader more readily if they know they will have a helper.

(2) *Of Group Participants*

The success of the discussion depends largely upon the group participants, NOT upon the leader. The responsibilities of the group participants in effective group discussion go far beyond the popular idea of "follow the leader and speak only when spoken to." Actually, group participants in successful groups share most of the responsibilities we have already listed for the leader. Here are some major responsibilities of group participants:

(a) *Before the Meeting*

    i) Prepare in advance to contribute to the discussion. This usually means reading materials about the topic, thinking about its personal significance, and jotting down questions and notes.

(b) *During the Discussion*

    i) Help adjust the goals and the outline when the opportunity is given at the start; don't just sit there if you do not understand them or if you wish to suggest a change.

    ii) Share your feelings and ideas on the topic; bring to bear facts and experience.

    iii) Help draw others into the discussion; don't expect the leader to direct the whole process.

    iv) Help other participants unstand each other; when someone else struggles, don't simply wait until you can tell what you think; do some asking and actively assist others to express themselves.

v) Alert the group when you feel they are "off the track"; help decide whether the digression is more important than the agreed-on topic.

vi) Listen actively and indicate your interest; avoid half-listening while planning what you will say next.

vii) Build on contributions that precede yours; help prevent others from "leapfrogging" someone's idea in order to present one he thinks is better.

viii) Actively help handle conflicts and problem situations that develop instead of depending upon the designated leader to do it. Effective group participants actually share the leader's job.

(c) *After the Discussion*

i) Give your opinion on the best topic for the next session.

ii) Express your opinions on the quality of the meeting and how it may be improved if an oral evaluation is conducted.

3. Training-Learning Method of Group Discussion

This type of group discussion is characterized here only briefly for purposes of clarification. Resources[1] and training programs are available to persons who wish to learn how to use this method.

a) Discussion has two purposes: (1) to discuss subject matter—problems relevant to Christian growth; and (2) to help participants learn how to learn together.

b) Discussion of subject matter is used as an opportunity for participants to practice serving in the roles of leader, observer, and responsible group participant. Interpersonal relations that develop during discussion are used as a means of learning more about self and how we relate to others as children of God. The process of interaction, as well as the content of the discussion, is considered a source of Christian learning.

c) Discussions are led by persons who volunteer to serve as designated leader or coleader for one or a few meetings at a time.

d) The sessions are directed by a teacher-leader often known as a "trainer." The trainer does *not* serve as discussion leader, except perhaps at the first session. Sometimes the trainer serves as *resource person* (source of information on the topic).

e) Discussion topics and learning goals are selected and worked out by the participants; such responsibilities are part of the learning task.

---

[1]Two chapters in *Design for Adult Education in the Church* by Paul Bergevin and John McKinley describe in detail one way to conduct this kind of program.

f) The trainer interrupts the discussion periodically to comment on the quality of the teamwork that is taking place.

g) Each session ends with an oral evaluation period during which participants identify obstacles to learning, assess their joint effort, and learn how it can be improved.

h) A *minimum* of eight to 10 sessions is usually necessary for a group to achieve most productive results.

This type of discussion has been used successfully with classes and groups that meet for 45 minutes to one hour each week. The experience is more satisfying if from one hour to one and one-half hours are available for each session.

Dangers

1. Dismissing the use of the blackboard or a chart pad as an unnecessary or childish device.

2. Letting the goal of discussion become that of compiling descriptive lists on the blackboard.

3. Assuming that purposes or goals need not be spelled out in visual terms and agreed on.

4. Setting goals that are too idealistic and long-range to give direction to the activity.

5. Continuing tendency to approach topics in abstract, impersonal terms; for example (a) by constantly comparing ideas of authorities on a topic in order to avoid personal feelings, and (b) by discussing only the words of a lesson, which often lead to testimonials in which participants simply repeat aloud that the lesson is true and cite instances to prove it.

6. Confusing discussion with argument or debate.

7. Trying to use group discussion as a directed teaching device to put over a preconceived viewpoint. This kind of operation calls for a method such as the lecture; discussion is exploration, not subtle inculcation of one viewpoint. Three indications of this kind of leadership are evident when:

a) A leader "doctors up" many of the participants' contributions to make them fit *his* outline or to point them toward "the truth" he is trying to emphasize.

b) A leader uses his power to prevent discussion from going along lines that won't lead to his preferred conclusion. He "overlooks" certain contributions, dismisses them quickly, or puts the group back on his track without asking whether they would prefer to stay on another one.

c) The leader will not deviate from *his* outline, but stoutly defends it as the only logical approach. He forgets he is a servant and that the discussion is theirs, not his. An academically logical outline is usually psychologically wrong for a group if it desires another approach to the topic. A teacher's outline and a discussion outline are two different things.

8. Tendency to let one or two so-called "natural leaders" or status persons be wholly responsible for such things as selecting topics, making outlines, and setting goals. These are group tasks, and the group will not openly and honestly evaluate something that is the result of the work of only a few. (Remember the significance of group evaluation, pp. 21-22.)

Chapter 7

The Seminar

The seminar is a teaching-learning procedure in which a group studies a subject under the direct guidance of a person qualified in that area. The teacher-leader plays a strong role in the planning of each session, leads the sessions himself, and provides lacking information; yet each session includes a period of free discussion by all participants. Actually the seminar combines individual research, preparation and presentation of reports by students, discussion of the reports by the entire seminar group, and directive comments and contributions by the teacher. In short, it is an informal class procedure in which both teacher and learners have certain defined responsibilities.

Uses

The seminar method can be readily adapted to many adult study activities in the church. The following examples are but a few of the situations in which the seminar could be used.

1. Church school classes that meet for at least 40 minutes. If the seminar method is being adapted to a church school class, some special problems must be dealt with:

a) The class should be in on the original decision to use this method, since it means changing an established pattern. Responsibilities of everyone involved should be reviewed and participants should agree to them.

b) If the lessons in a quarterly are to be used to define the content area of seminar sessions, each seminar topic should be a problem sufficiently chiselled out and defined so that the student who reports can present findings and conclusions that are his own. This defining will very likely have to be done by the teacher well in advance.

c) Before the seminar sessions begin, the class should have a chance to talk over the topics suggested by the teacher so they will understand why he thinks the topics are significant.

d) Very little, if any, classtime should be allotted by the teacher to advisory comments to persons whose reports are to be given the following session. This must be handled in weekday personal conferences.

2. Bible study groups that meet during the week.

3. Special-interest series of adult classes conducted periodically, often during certain seasons in the church year.

4. Programs of fellowship organizations which devote part of each meeting to an educational activity.

A Program Pattern

Here are two illustrative time schemes that point out how the seminar can be adapted to a 45-minute schedule and to a one-and-one-half-hour situation. The brief descriptions of events will help you visualize the pattern of activity:

10:00 A.M. Teacher presents *brief* historical or conceptual background for the report; reminds participants of their responsibilities.

10:05 Participant reads written report.

10:15 Either teacher or reporter leads discussion of report, based on questions asked by participants; teacher encourages questions, makes contributions, asks leading questions, answers questions briefly.

10:30 Teacher comments upon significant aspects of the report, presents relevant information that has not come to light, and presents an organized summary.

10:45 Conclusion, reminder of next assignment.

• ◆ •

7:30 P.M. Teacher presents background information to prepare for report; reminds participants of their responsibilities.

7:40 Participant-reporter reads written report; other participants take notes, jot down questions.

7:55 Reporter or teacher leads forum discussion based on questions raised by participants.

8:25 Teacher comments upon report; presents significant information that is needed; presents an organized summary.

8:45 Teacher, stimulates participants to prepare for next session, presents "lead-in" questions, com-

ments on significance, reminds them of reading assignments.

9:00   Conclusion.

Desirable Conditions

1. Since the seminar is intended to be rather informal within its organized structure, it is an advantage
for the group to sit around tables in a circular or
rectangular arrangement.

2. The blackboard is usually not used as much as
in group discussion, but many teachers find it to be an
effective visual teaching tool.

3. The size of the room should be appropriate to
the size of the group.

4. The concept of the seminar room as a study center is often helpful. This means that the room should
be provided with a library of appropriate reference
books and reading materials which participants can
use there or check out; a file of past reports given by
participants, note paper, extra pencils, and reading
tables.

Procedures

1. Responsibilities of Teacher-leader

This person should be chosen for his knowledge of
the subject, his ability to plan and direct the writing
of reports, and his ability to impart his knowledge
helpfully.

a) *At the Preliminary Meeting*

The seminar method is usually used for a *series*
of sessions. It is not thought of as a one-shot deal,

but as a way of studying systematically during a number of sessions some subject area of interest to those who will participate. Thus it is usually advantageous to hold a preliminary meeting in advance of the first actual seminar session. The teacher has the following tasks to perform at this meeting:

(1) Present an outline of the content that will be covered in the sessions. Each participant should receive a copy. Give a thumbnail sketch of the content.

(2) Explain the purpose of the sessions and the significance of the field of study from the teacher's viewpoint.

(3) Explain how each seminar session will be conducted, what will be expected of the participants, and what they can expect from the teacher.

(4) Make available to each participant a list of readings that clearly point out specific chapters, page numbers, verses, etc., for each session, with directions for obtaining these resources.

(5) Get some participants to volunteer several sessions in advance to give reports on significant aspects of the subject area as determined by the teacher in consultation with the participants.

b) *Before the Meeting*

(1) If necessary, help the person who is preparing the next report; do not write the report for him, but help him organize it,

find appropriate resource materials, and hold it within time limits.

(2) Review the area to be covered in the seminar session and note down major points to be covered in the summary.

(3) Develop some leading questions that can be used to focus the session on major issues, relate it to Christian living, and draw out participation.

(4) Create a few "lead-in" questions that will stimulate interest in, and guide preparation for, the session following the one you are preparing to attend.

c) *During the Meeting*

(1) Start on time.

(2) Remind participants of their responsibilities during the session.

(3) Avoid interrupting the report (it is sometimes necessary to have an agreed-on signal to indicate impersonally when the report should be drawn to a close).

(4) Help spark discussion of the report, but avoid answering questions that others can answer; provide useful comments without making a series of speeches at this point; raise questions and facilitate discussion of learning problems revealed by participants.

(5) Comment on the significant points in the report and present a summary indicating how the report and what it covered fits into the larger subject area of which it is a part.

(6) Stimulate enthusiasm and participation for the next session; give some "lead-in" questions to guide the reading.

(7) Review sources where written materials may be secured.

(8) End on time.

d) *After the Meeting*

(1) Check to make sure next report-giver has his assignment straight.

(2) Offer to assist the next report-giver in organizing his report.

(3) Make sure written resources are available for those who wish to check them out of the church library.

2. Responsibilities of Participants

To clarify the major duties of seminar participants they are listed in the Program Pattern on page 70. It is hoped that this will facilitate advance preparation by everyone concerned and also define their roles.

a) *Before the Meeting*

(1) One group participant (sometimes a pair) organizes a written report. The report should present informed findings on the topic; but it should be more than a digest and recitation of information gleaned from authorities. Although facts and opinions should form its basis, the report-giver should summarize the significance of these facts.

(2) The other participants prepare to participate orally by reading appropriate

materials and thinking about the topic before attending the seminar meeting.

b) *During the Meeting*

(1) Listen to the report, jot down questions, and prepare to discuss.

(2) Offer your ideas and opinions during the discussion.

(3) Ask for clarification when you do not understand what is said.

(4) Help others to express themselves.

(5) Express disagreement with ideas (not persons) when you feel it; try to clarify the basis of the disagreement instead of trying

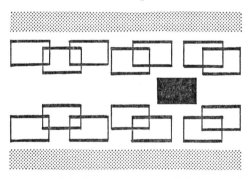

to label some person "right" and another "wrong."

Dangers

A common misuse of the seminar method occurs when it becomes a report followed by a lecture. The seminar is tant aspect of the seminar is the working together of students and teacher as an informal group.

Chapter 8

The Colloquy

The colloquy is a learning-group method usually used by groups of from 25 to 75 persons. It must be adapted carefully to the learning task at hand, since it is a highly flexible tool.

Basically the colloquy is a pattern of purposeful, cooperative interaction between three units of participants—an audience, a panel of resource persons, and a panel of audience representatives. The interaction is controlled by a moderator. The audience representatives present a problem or initiate questions which originated in the audience. The resource persons present information designed to help answer the questions, and members of the audience participate actively whenever feasible, under the direction of the moderator.

Techniques have been developed to handle such problems as getting audience representatives, arming them with questions that originate in the audience, and using the colloquy with large audiences. These problems are discussed briefly later in this chapter.

Uses

The choice of method depends mainly upon the tasks and goals of the specific meeting and the resources available. The colloquy applies in some situations where other methods are not adequate.

    1. It can be used in many cases as an effective method of following up a speech, a symposium, or a panel presentation. (See Chapter 10 for samples of this program pattern.)

    2. It can be used effectively by a group which has been studying some problem or need area and has accumulated a fund of questions or issues they need to clarify with trained resource persons.

    3. It can be used effectively to arouse interest in a problem area and in a series of follow-up meetings.

    4. It can be used to illustrate the value of two educational principles:

        ℘ molding a program to the problems and needs recognized by the participants.

        ℘ using resource persons at the moment they are needed.

A Program Pattern

Here we present one basic program pattern for the use of the colloquy and two common variations that are frequently used. The colloquy used in combination with other methods is described in Chapter 10.

The colloquy as a major vehicle requires from 45 minutes to one and one-half hours of program time. Usually the program is composed of three units:

    1. A meaningful introduction, by chairman or moderator, in which the tasks, goals, and mechanics

of the meeting are reviewed briefly and the audience is broken down into small groups of usually six to ten persons, each group being assigned a certain meeting place near by. (See "the Buzz Group technique" in Chapter 10.)

2. Small-group activity for 10 to 15 minutes; audience members develop questions on the given topic area.

3. The colloquy proper; one audience representative from each small group sits as a member of the audience panel, whose members take turns submitting the questions from the small groups, one at a time. The resource experts deal with the questions one at a time, and the audience is encouraged to comment and ask additional questions before moving to the next question from the audience panel.

The vital part of the colloquy is not so much the questions asked by the audience representatives, or the answers handed down by the authorities: most vital is the *active clarification* by the audience of the *significance* of the informational material they receive from the authorities. In an effective colloquy the audience often does as much talking as the resource experts do. This is desirable, since it is the participants' job actively to discover personal meaning and obstacles to understanding. The resource persons can assist best when the participant helps him understand how best to go about it.

Here is a program outline of a typical colloquy that is designed to last one hour and 15 minutes for 30 to 40 persons.

8:00 P.M. Chairman opens with prayer;

introduces the three resource persons and the problem area, e.g., "Helping Children Grow as Christians";

reviews task and goals of the meeting;

explains the colloquy method briefly;

divides audience into four small groups by having them count off by 4's;

sets task for small groups: to develop one question in each of three areas (overcoming obstacles to Christian growth in the home, in the school, in the community or neighborhood).

8:10   Four small groups meet, get volunteer recorders, and develop questions in the three areas.

8:25   Audience regathers (recorders from small groups form as audience panel, up front, each with his list of questions);

questions are submitted one at a time to the resource persons;

audience and resource persons explore each question together with the help of the moderator.

9:15   Summary by chairman.

Closing prayer.

Refreshment period.

Variations of the Colloquy

A common variation of the colloquy as outlined above is often used. This adaptation omits the step of getting questions from the audience by the small-group method. Instead, a planning committee meets a week or two in advance of the colloquy and identifies a list of key problems—questions that will be put into the hands of the audience representatives. The audience representatives must also be chosen well in advance of the meeting.

One possible advantage of this procedure is that it devotes all of the program time to working on the questions; but caution is necessary since the questions may seem "rigged" and be unrepresentative. One way to anticipate this shortcoming is to have members of the planning committee actually solicit questions from potential audience members several days in advance.

One other variation of the colloquy has been used, particularly with large audiences. In this procedure it is anticipated that few audience persons will participate from the floor. Thus the panel of audience representation not only initiates questions, but comments freely on the experts' answers. They become the audience on a small scale and take on its normal function in the colloquy. While this is a kind of "split-panel" discussion, or perhaps an interview type of presentation rather than a true colloquy, some circumstances justify its use.

Desirable Conditions

1. When arranging the physical set-up, it is helpful to separate the two panels slightly and place them

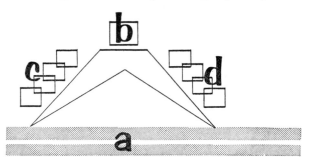

at approximately right angles to each other, with the moderator at the corner of the V. Tables for the two panels are usually appreciated.

2. Resource persons should be contacted well ahead of time and told what will be expected of them. They usually need to be reminded that long speeches are out of place, and that questioning and clarification will take place throughout the meeting as audience members and audience representatives see the need.

Responsibilities

1. Of the Moderator

The moderator is not a teacher or one who foments or referees a debate. The business of learning together is a co-operative, not a competitive, venture. He is a key person in the successful use of the colloquy. He co-ordinates the questions from the audience panel, the remarks of the resource experts, and the questions and comments from the audience. Since *everyone* at the meeting is potentially an active contributor, it is essential in large groups for the moderator to exert somewhat formal control such as

℄ encouraging audience participants to raise their hands when they wis'ı to comment

℄ giving the flooɾ to one person at a time.

Here are some specific duties the moderator usually is expected to perform:

a) Set a relaxed atmosphere at the start; humor helps. In the introductory remarks, describe the mechanics of the meeting and what is expected of the audience; mention the task and goals of the meeting; introduce the resource persons.

b) Encourage audience participation repeatedly during the colloquy; we are all fairly unaccustomed to continuous opportunities to participate along with resource persons.

c) Rephrase and clarify vague contributions.

d) Repeat questions not loudly and clearly stated and direct them to appropriate resource person; try to get a nod or signal of willingness from the one who desires to answer the question.

e) When drawing in audience participants, give preference to those who have not yet made a contribution.

2. Of the audience representatives

The audience representatives also play a key role in the successful use of this method. The audience representatives *never* serve in the capacity of resource experts. They sit up front beside the moderator for three major reasons:

a) Through audience representatives, persons in the audience can identify themselves positively with the platform and its experts; they help overcome the audience feeling of "they are different from me; they don't know my problems."

b) The use of audience representatives stimulates active listening and increased verbal participation by the audience.

c) Audience representatives localize specific responsibility for initiating new questions whenever they are needed.

Dangers

1. Audience members may tend to sit, as usual, and listen to the platform people "perform" for them. Moderators have found it helpful to interrupt the meeting briefly to remind the audience members that they may signal the moderator whenever they have a contribution to make.

2. Resource persons may forget their role and launch into long speeches. Moderators sometimes find it necessary to interject questions during slight pauses in order to redirect the process.

3. In highly vocal groups and with highly controversial topics, the meeting can get out of hand unless the moderator maintains control.

4. The moderator should talk with the audience representatives briefly so they will know what is expected of them. Sometimes it is feasible to arrange with them to submit questions of their own that arise during the meeting—particularly if it turns out that the audience is fairly unresponsive.

5. A committee of those who will be participants should help plan the program. What will occur during the meeting should be outlined step by step in the planning session. At least a committee of the participants should have a hand in identifying the problem or subject area to be explored in the colloquy.

Chapter 9

The Panel and the Symposium

The panel and the symposium are two distinctly different educational methods. Similar in some respects, both methods are used to present opinions and information to an audience or a class; both methods employ a panel of resource persons; neither method in its pure form makes use of oral audience participation. The chief difference between them lies in the manner in which the resource persons make their presentation.

The Panel

The panel is a presentation method in which a group of (usually) four to eight qualified persons sit in front of an audience and hold an informal, orderly conversation on a given topic with the help of a moderator. At its best, the panel presentation is a small-group discussion conducted on-stage, so to speak. The panel members do not make prepared speeches (as so often happens), but talk informally to each other, while the audience "listens in."

Uses

The general uses listed here are only clues to point toward possibilities. Often it is necessary to use a combination of various methods to accomplish the task of a meeting. See Chapter 10 for ways of modifying the panel.

1. To present and explore learning problems of religious education common to the group or audience.

2. To follow up a film presentation with interpretative comments that assist in understanding its significance.

3. To present representative reactions to (or interpretations of) a given problem, subject, or topic.

If the task is to present various professional interpretations of a given topic, problem, or text, then specially qualified resource persons are often required on the panel. But there is much to be said for having willing lay persons discuss problems of adult religious education in front of other lay persons. This not only helps legitimize a lay-language approach to adult religious education, but also helps listeners recognize that other persons feel as they do and struggle with similar problems. In Bible classes the panel discussion often focuses on the significance of a passage or the exploration of a problem revealed in a passage of scripture.

The Symposium

The symposium is a presentation method in which (usually) two to four qualified resource persons present brief speeches on various aspects of a given subject. The symposium is mainly a method of dispensing information and informed opinions. As in the case of the panel, the symposium has certain advantages: short speeches tend to be well organized and purposeful, the pet ideas of a single speaker are not emphasized, and different ideas given by different persons tend to promote active listening.

The general uses of the symposium fit the same situations listed above for the use of the panel. However, it should be said that the symposium tends to be a more formal method of presentation. Each five- or 10- or 15-minute speech given in the symposium is a formally organized unit given by one person. In the panel presentation, each problem or question is discussed by *all* the resource persons, so that the audience hears a spectrum of opinions and viewpoints as the presentation unfolds.

Before choosing the panel or the symposium as the single, major vehicle for a meeting, the planners should consider the possibilities of using some form of panel-forum or symposium-forum (see Chapter 10).

Desirable Conditions

A preliminary meeting with resource persons is needed to spell out responsibilities and topic areas to be developed. In the case of a panel, the presentation should not be rehearsed since this prevents spontaneity.

Responsibilities

1. In a panel presentation, the moderator usually
   a) introduces the topic
   b) co-ordinates the panel discussion
   c) presents a final summary.

(See the duties of the moderator outlined in Chapters 4 and 8.)

2. Symposium speeches and panel presentations should grow out of problems and needs recognized by the audience or group involved. A committee of them should plan the meeting well in advance.

3. Audience members should do some thinking and reading in advance if they are to derive the most benefit from a panel or symposium presentation. They will be most likely to do this if they have had a hand in shaping and planning the program.

Dangers

1. Not all resource persons can operate well in panel presentations.

2. Do not assume that it is unnecessary for the meeting chairman or the moderator to meet with the resource persons before the presentation in order to clarify the procedures, set limits as to topic coverage, and review responsibilities.

Chapter 10

Modifying Panel, Symposium, and Speech Programs

Some kind of active audience participation is often needed to make speech and panel presentations most effective. These opportunities for audience participation are sometimes called forum[1] periods. Many combinations of methods are used to give audiences an opportunity to "talk back" after a presentation.

Reasons for Forum Participation

1. Adults tend to resist the role of "learner," and this role is made painfully clear when there is no opportunity to talk back. We need to assert the independence we associate with our adulthood; forum periods provide these opportunities.

2. Adults sometimes resist listening to a teacher or any expert because "he is not like me," or "he doesn't understand my problems." Interaction between audience and platform can help break down these feelings over a period of time.

---

[1]Forum is used here in the general sense of an audience-participation period. It is not to be confused with the specific group method called the forum, which is not described in this booklet.

3. Only through continued participation will we learn to trust our colearners.

4. Adult learners need the support of knowing that fellow learners have similar misunderstandings, problems, and difficulties in making new learning meaningful. This support can come through forum participation.

The Open Forum

This is the simplest of all follow-up procedures, yet it is perhaps the most difficult one in which to get active oral participation in a large group. After a presentation the open forum begins when the moderator says, "Now are there any questions from the audience?" Persons with real questions seldom stand up and express them openly, particularly timid persons. One way to avoid this pitfall is to

have the audience members write out their questions on cards. These cards are collected and taken to the moderator who reads the questions aloud and encourages the resource person(s) to deal with them. The open forum is usually most effective with groups of fewer than 50 persons who already know each other fairly well. It can often be made more effective by using buzz groups or the reaction panel to stimulate forum participation.

The Buzz Group Technique

The buzz group technique is a transitional device participants can use to bridge the gap between a presentation and a forum period for clarifying the presentation in personal terms.

It is one way to get maximum oral participation from an audience after a presentation, such as film, a lecture, a role play, a panel, or a symposium. The basic idea is to involve the audience actively by

℘ breaking it into small discussion groups of usually four to eight persons,

℘ assigning to these groups a discussion task to be accomplished in five to 15 minutes, and

℘ reassembling the audience, hearing the buzz group reports and conducting a large-group participation period, usually with the help of resource persons.

Program planners ought to answer at least three related questions before deciding definitely to use buzz groups:

1. Will the audience need to participate?

2. If it is needed, what kind of participation will be needed? Will the tasks of the buzz groups be legitimate?

3. Can the results of the buzz groups be used effectively?

Procedures

1. Give clear, specific directions for forming groups quickly. Some planners take care of this by

numbering the chairs, or by giving each participant a tag with a group number on it when he first shows up for the meeting. Sometimes it is feasible to count off (by 5's if you need five groups, by 6's if you need six groups, and so forth). Frequently, if the audience has movable chairs, persons in the first row can turn their chairs and form buzz groups with persons in the second row; the same with rows 3 and 4, etc. (This was done successfully with 200 persons recently in a gymnasium, with the assistance of four ushers.)

2. Give a specific time limit. Sound a warning gong if the groups are in one room, but send messengers to call time if groups are scattered in various rooms.

3. Describe *specific* tasks for the buzz groups to accomplish: "Identify at least five points that need clarifying" or "List the three most important questions which this lecture raises" or "What do you consider the three best solutions to the problem you have heard discussed?" It is helpful to have the tasks written out on cards, on a blackboard, or on newsprint.

4. Suggest some ways the buzz groups can quickly determine who will serve as recorder, such as, a volunteer; the oldest person; one whose last name begins with the letter nearest A, or Z.

5. Always use the recorded results of the buzz groups when the audience regathers. Never hear some group reports and not others.

In the "program pattern" section at the conclusion of this chapter four instances are given in which buzz groups are used in combination with other methods.

The Reaction Panel Technique

With large classes or audiences this procedure has been used after a presentation such as a speech, a panel, a symposium, or a film.

The reaction panel is a group of three to six persons, usually chosen beforehand as representative members of the audience. After the presentation, these persons go to the platform and hold a five- or 10-minute panel discussion in which they react to the opinions and information given in the presentation. They do reveal

℄ what they understand it to mean,

℄ what they did not understand,

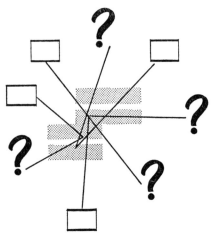

℄ what questions they now have. After their remarks, the resource persons usually try to clarify the questions, and if time allows the audience is drawn into an open forum under the direction of the moderator.

Uses

1. To stimulate active participation in an open forum that follows.

2. To take the place of a forum when little time will be available after the presentation.

This procedure is most effective when the resource persons are patient and not defensive. If they interrupt the panel to answer questions raised, the panel members may feel on the spot.

The Screening Panel Technique

The screening panel procedure is one way of making fairly sure that a panel, a speaker, or a group of symposium speakers will deal with problems and needs which a class or audience recognizes.

Procedures

1. A problem-need area is identified at least a week in advance by a committee of planners, who get appropriate resource person(s) and secure three to six audience representatives for an audience panel.

2. The meeting begins with a 10- to 15-minute panel discussion by the audience representatives, who reveal informally the problems of understanding in the topic area. The resource person(s) listens to the panel and builds a presentation tailored to the needs of the group.

3. The resource person(s) makes the presentation (speech, panel, or symposium).

4. Some kind of forum participation follows, if needed.

In one variation of this technique, the screening panel members are not chosen in advance of the meeting. The meeting begins with a 10-minute buzz group period, during which the class or audience is broken into groups of five to 10 persons. Each group forms questions they want answered and sends one representative to sit on the screening panel and present their questions and problems. Steps 3 and 4, above, then follow.

The Colloquy as a Follow-Up Device

Chapter 8 describes the use of colloquy as a vehicle for a total meeting. The colloquy can also be used in combination with presentation methods such as the speech, the panel, or the symposium. To illustrate these possibilities the following program pattern is offered. *The reader should review Chapter 8 to understand the mechanics of the colloquy.*

7:30 PM Chairman's introduction describes tasks, goals, mechanics of meeting and introduces resource persons.

7:40 Three symposium presentations (or perhaps a panel presentation) are made.

8:10 Chairman breaks audience into buzz groups to develop questions and reactions.

8:25 Colloquy is conducted by moderator (one member of each buzz group serves on the audience panel; three symposium speakers serve as re-

source panel; open forum held on each question
as it is dealt with.

9:00   Chairman closes meeting.

Some Program Patterns

In order to illustrate the principles of using combinations
of various methods in the same meeting, a few examples
are presented below in outline form. Program planners
must remember that methods are not combined for the
sake of mere variety. A given combination should be used
because it seems to be the best way of reaching the goal of
the meeting.

It is assumed that the reader has digested Chapters 4-9
of this book. This is necessary if he is to understand some
of the terms used here, and how one portion of a meeting
would flow into the next one.

#1 – Screening panel (10
       min.)
    – Speech (20 min.)
    – Buzz groups (15
       min.)
    – Group reports and
       open forum (30
       min.)
#2 – Buzz groups (10
       min.)
    – Screening panel (10
       min.)
    – Speech (20 min.)
    – Open forum (20
       min.)

#3 – Speech, or sympo-
       sium or panel (20-
       30 min.)
    – Buzz groups (15
       min.)
    – Group reports and
       open forum (30
       min.)
#4 – Panel, or speech, or
       Symposium (20-30
       min.)
    – Buzz groups (10
       min.)
    – Reaction panel (10
       min.)

- Open forum (20 min.)

\#5 – Panel, or speech, or symposium (30 min.)
- Reaction panel (15 min.)

- Open forum (30 min.)

\#6 – Symposium, speech, or panel (30 min.)
- Buzz groups (15 min.)
- Colloquy (30 min.)

\#7 – Symposium (30 min.)
- Colloquy (30 min.)

Obviously there are countless combinations of resources and methods available. We have not even mentioned films, role plays, and many other resources and presentations that could be worked into a program pattern.